GLASGOW

Photographs by
Colin Baxter

Text by
Ian Mitchell

www.lomondbooks.com

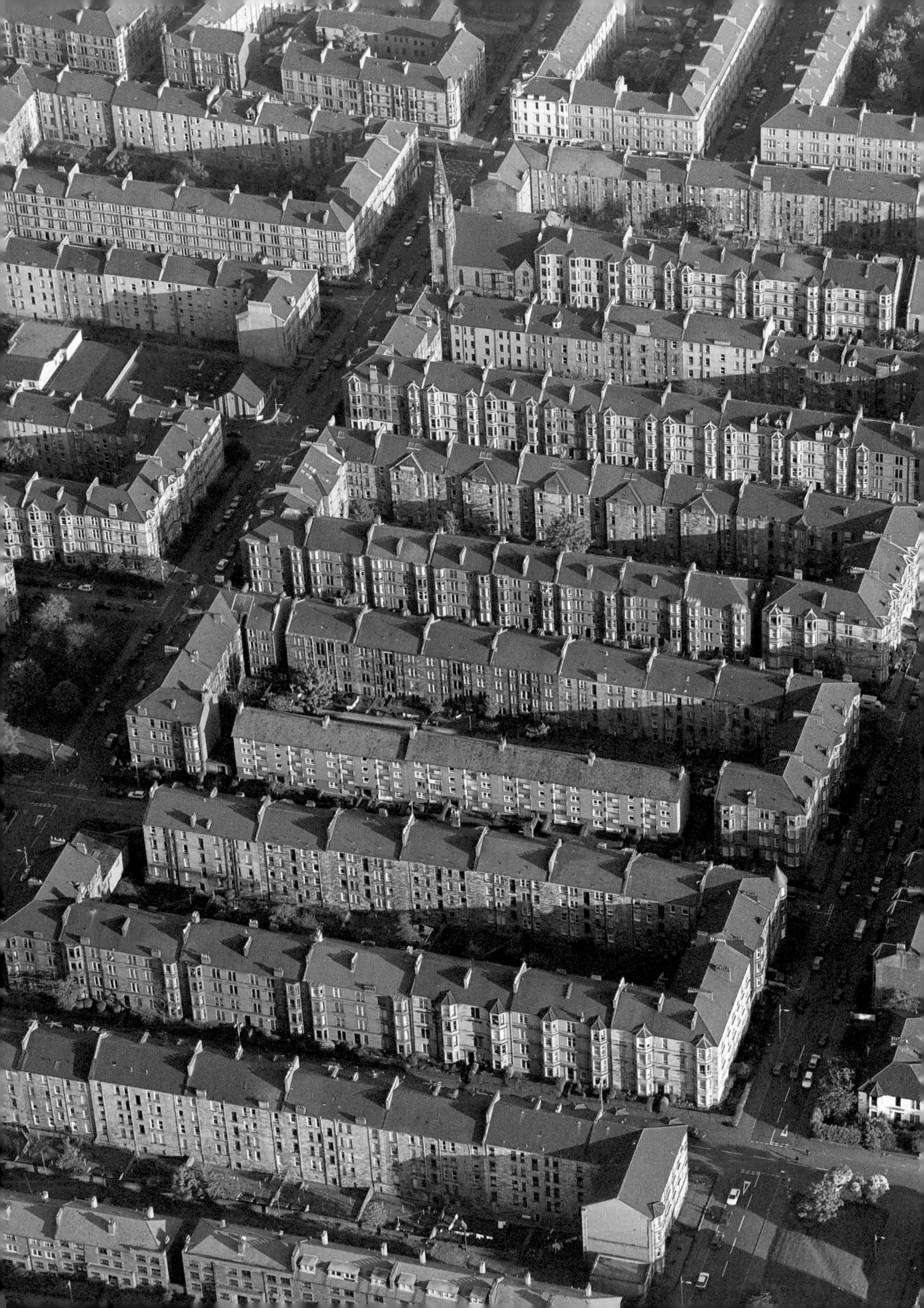

GLASGOW

'The greatest Victorian city in the world'. That was how the late Sir John Betjeman, Poet Laureate and expert on Victoriana, saw central Glasgow, a view that is perhaps difficult to reconcile with the panorama of the city presented from most of the approach roads before their descent from the surrounding hills: a forest of high-rise blocks rising like stalagmites out of the bowl in which Glasgow lies. For the visitor arriving by rail, however, who emerges from the huge iron and glass vault of Queen Street Station directly on to George Square, or from Central Station into Gordon Street, to come face to face with the massive pilasters and domes of the Grosvenor Building (originally a warehouse, later a sumptuous restaurant and banqueting hall which gave it its name, but now, like so many city centre properties everywhere, given over to offices), the impact is immediate, and the poet's admiration can be readily appreciated. Just round the corner from the Grosvenor, in Union Street, stands, in

OLD AND NEW
Looking across the River Clyde to St Andrew's Cathedral and the St Enoch Centre.

FROM THE AIR (opposite). Typical red and yellow sandstone tenements, with some grey concrete replacements, in the central suburb of Dennistoun.

THE CITY CENTRE
Grid-pattern from above.

DECORATIVE TILES
(opposite) in a tenement
entrance, or 'close'.

THE CLYDESDALE
BANK, in Buchanan
Street.

typically breathtaking contrast, a reconstruction of the Ca' d'Oro in Venice. Where to turn next? It hardly matters, since on every one of the city centre's grid-pattern streets, Greek stands cheek-by-jowl with Gothic, Venetian with Egyptian, Art Nouveau and Art Deco with Renaissance, with smatterings of Italianate and Scottish Baronial and other exotica in between.

The sum total is far from the hotchpotch it might at first sound. By eschewing the more garish excesses of Victorian taste which raise eyebrows in some other cities, the creators of central Glasgow succeeded, by good planning or by good luck, in achieving that harmony which can arise from such diversity. This becomes clear

during any stroll around the area; one of the most striking examples is the walk from George Square westwards along St Vincent Place and up the steep rise of St Vincent Street to the top of one of the many hills, or drumlins, on which the heart of Glasgow is built. It takes in the façades decorated with columns, mouldings and sculptures, and a cornucopia of towers, turrets, cupolas, cornices, balustrades and statues embellishing the roof-lines.

There are no royal palaces here, few witnesses to Scotland's turbulent past, its almost constant struggles with its larger neighbour to the south or the dark deeds committed by its feuding clans; these are to be found elsewhere, in the Highlands to the North or in that 'other place' to the East (the rivalry between Glasgow and Edinburgh is well documented, and illustrated by countless anecdotes and barbed asides). Still, palaces and monuments there are aplenty, celebrating instead man's ingenuity, invention and industry. By their very nature, some such monuments to Mammon are perhaps more transient than royal abodes, more readily overtaken by the developments of their particular kind of history, and most of the heavy engineering relics of Glasgow's industrial past, when it was the Second City of the Empire and workshop of the world, such as the Clydeside shipyards and the locomotive-building works, have disappeared. Fortunately, they have taken with them a great deal of their inevitable extensions, the social disaster areas of the slums and the pall of smoke which left every building in the city coated with layers of soot and grime. It was only

SHIPYARD CRANES are a reminder of the age of Glasgow's industrial prowess. The Finnieston Crane (above) once loaded steam locomotives on to ships. Over eighty shipyards once lined the Clyde; three remain.

IN THE CITY CENTRE (above), the City Chambers and other Victorian domes and cupolas still challenge the cranes and the tower blocks which elsewhere seem to dominate the skyline: near St George's Cross (below).

well into the 1970s that the hidden glories of the red and yellow sandstone – a trademark of the city – were revealed once more.

In the post-war years, the City Council's first priority was the redevelopment of a city which had become notorious for its slums, the worst legacy of the industrial boom of the Victorian era. The Gorbals area, just south of the river and only ten minutes' walk from the magnificence of the City Chambers, had become a byword for an inhuman environment and all its attendant social ills. Worse than that, the slums became synonymous with Glasgow as a whole, indelibly colouring the perceptions of many outsiders. Vast areas of Glasgow's housing consisted of sandstone tenements, in the West End mainly three storeys high and with spacious, high-ceilinged rooms, but in the East End consisting of four storeys of cramped, two-

roomed flats without internal sanitation. The former had been constructed for the rising middle-class, while the latter arose on a 'throw 'em up and pack 'em in' principle to house the huge influx of cheap labour from the Highlands and Ireland. By the end of the 1950s, they were at last recognised as totally unfit for human habitation.

Glasgow has never been a city to do things by halves, and so the spirit

THE GORBALS, across the Clyde from the city centre. Here, as in many of Glasgow's suburbs, the 'high flats' now characterise an area once tightly packed with dark, sub-standard tenements.

of the new age, a combination of 'if it's old, it has to go' and the strange determination to build the highest flats in Europe, led to a programme of blanket demolition. While this drastic policy seemed, at the time, the only feasible solution for many areas such as the Gorbals, it resulted in the destruction not merely of housing stock but of whole tight-knit communities which still thrived in some of the one-time villages long since sucked in by the growing city. The population of these areas was hastily 'decanted' into huge new peripheral developments, working-class dormitories, most of them virtually devoid of basic social amenities like shops and pubs – an oversight that has been redressed only in recent years – or into New Towns such as East Kilbride and Cumbernauld, far from its natural, urban habitat, and, finally, in the 1960s, into enormous complexes of tower-blocks which induced the very opposite of the old community spirit.

The result of the headlong drive for renewal was sometimes the replacement of horizontal slums by vertical ones, using cheap materials and hasty, shoddy building techniques, with bright

BAIRD HALL, now a Strathclyde University hall of residence, was built in 1938, for the Empire Exhibition, as the Beresford Hotel. Its art deco frontage stands out above Sauchiehall Street.

sandstone giving way to grey concrete. A number of these new blocks have already been demolished only three decades after construction, to be outlived by tenements like those they replaced. Out of the very excesses of these policies, however, grew the first seeds of opposition, with the foundation in 1963 of the New Glasgow Society, which recognised the need for redevelopment, but proposed that it should be based on the use and refurbishment, rather than the obliteration, of the old Victorian city. Whole areas of tenement properties, once earmarked for demolition to make way for motorways, were instead redeveloped, street by street, their interiors ripped out, leaving only the façades, and rebuilt to accommodate larger flats. Then, under the impetus of the 1956 Clean Air Act, the industrial grime was sandblasted off the sandstone exteriors to reveal a city which had, until the mid sixties, presented a uniformly black face, and now, in the slanting sun of a summer evening, glows like some Mediterranean conurbation.

Where the city centre was concerned. the story of what might *not* have been takes an even more dramatic turn. This remarkable testimony to the Victorians' eclecticism came within an ace of being denied to the present-day visitor. Here, however, the escape from the bulldozer was more complete. A radical plan for remodelling the inner city proposed the construction of a motorway ring and the replacement of everything within that ring by high-rise commercial buildings – Chicago-on-Clyde! The scrapping of this project in 1959, very much at the last minute of the eleventh hour, was a reprieve for which everyone since then, inhabitants and visitors alike, can be thankful.

The Victorians were by no means the first to leave their imprint on the face of Glasgow. Nevertheless, the seeker after relics of medieval times, for example, is doomed to disappointment. Nothing remains of those early ages other than those parts of the Cathedral dating from the thirteenth century and, close by, Glasgow's oldest surviving dwelling-house, Provand's Lordship. Built in 1471 as the Manse for the adjacent St Nicholas Hospital, a hospice for 'a priest and twelve old men', it subsequently fulfilled a variety of purposes and today is a museum. The name derives from the Prebend, or Provan, of the parish of Balornock, who was also housed there. It would be wrong to see in this dearth of ancient relics an indication that Glasgow's more recent tendency to sweep the old ruthlessly aside to make way for the new has its roots deep in the past. Instead, it illustrates the paradox that, while the history of Glasgow as a settlement is indeed a long one, that of Glasgow as a significant community is, by contrast, remarkably brief.

'Let Glasgow Flourish by the Preaching of the Word' was the original motto on the Glasgow coat-of-arms. Here, on the banks of the Molendinar Burn, in AD 543, St Kentigern (the name means 'noble lord') or, as Glasgow prefers to call its patron saint, Mungo ('dear one'), built a wooden church, in which he himself was later buried. For six centuries after that, the little fishing village seems to have existed in a vacuum until a new, stone church

WINE BAR in Queen Street.

'THE WAVERLEY'
Lone survivor of the once fierce competition for passengers on the Clyde, the paddle-steamer now offers summer cruises.

VICTORIAN SPLENDOUR
The former Liverpool, London and Globe Building at the corner of St Vincent Street and Hope Street, a junction which has been described as architecturally 'the most spectacular in Glasgow'.

CATHEDRAL SQUARE (opposite), relaid in the early 1990s. A model provides a view of the whole surrounding area.

was dedicated on the same site in 1136 by Bishop John Achaius in the presence of King David I, who also commissioned the Borders abbeys (and doomed his successors and indeed his country to a chronic shortage of funds). In 1175, burgh status was conferred on this market town and bishop's residence, which consisted of no more than two streets – roughly, today's High Street and Argyle Street.

The Cathedral in its present form was completed in the fifteenth century, with Provand's Lordship forming part of the complex. Just down the road, the original University, the 'Old College', was founded in 1451, and so Glasgow became a seat of religion and learning, but never of the nobility or the military.

This life of contemplation and scholarship continued until well into the eighteenth century, when the transition from quiet market town to Scotland's largest city began. Glasgow's geographical situation had hitherto proved something of a handicap, since practically all of the nation's foreign trade was conducted from ports on the east coast, which were closer to Europe, the Baltic States in particular. Whatever reservations many Scots had – and still have –

regarding the Treaty of Union in 1707, it did open up free trade within the United Kingdom and removed the restrictions that had previously been imposed on Scottish trade with the English colonies in the Americas, thus providing the impetus for Glasgow to flourish by other means than 'by the Preaching of the Word', (which was soon to disappear from the motto). It rapidly became the hub of the trade in rum, sugar and, most significantly of all, tobacco from the Carolinas, Virginia and Maryland. What Daniel Defoe described as 'a large stately and well-built city, standing on a plain in a manner four-square, and the five principal streets are the fairest for breadth and the finest built I have ever seen in one city together... one of the cleanliest, most beautiful and best built cities in Great Britain' saw its population double from somewhere between ten and fifteen thousand at the turn of the century to 28,000 in 1763, and rise to 67,000 by the late 1780s.

GLASGOW UNIVERSITY at dusk.

The outbreak of the American War of Independence in 1775 struck hard at the tobacco trade, leaving many notable citizens, and indeed the city itself, on the brink of ruin. Yet out of that ruin there quickly arose another thriving industry, manufacturing and processing first linen, then cotton. By the time King Cotton's demise was imminent, James Watt (1736-1819), ignoring the old adage that 'a watched kettle never boils', had developed his steam engine and this, combined with the opening up for full exploitation of the vast mineral wealth of the city's hinterland, meant that the next transition stage, to heavy industry, followed more or less without the trauma of 'boom-and-slump'.

Those who made their fortunes from the tobacco trade, the

THE RIVER CLYDE, CITY CENTRE (opposite) flows westwards past Glasgow Green, and beneath many bridges, towards the sites of former shipyards at Finnieston and beyond.

THE HIGH STREET, looking south towards Glasgow Cross, with the Tolbooth Steeple prominent at the junction with Argyle Street.

'Tobacco Lords' or 'Barons' as they are also known, put their profits to good use. Not only did they establish a banking industry as well as new factories for the already burgeoning linen trade, but they put much of their money back into the fabric of the city in the form of streets of noble Palladian mansions reflecting their wealth and status. The old Glasgow, which had huddled around the High Street from the Cathedral, down past the University to Glasgow Cross, the Tolbooth Steeple and the Trongate, spread rapidly westwards. Within a few decades, many elegant town houses were constructed. One of the most remarkable is the mansion which William Cunninghame of Lainshaw, a rich Tobacco Lord, had built in 1778 in the middle of a large garden. In 1827, it was to become the centrepiece of a particularly striking example of that peculiarly Glasgow feature, a tight square laid out around an imposing central building, very often a church. This was to be Royal Exchange Square. In time, Cunninghame's mansion was to undergo various changes, not only architecturally, with the addition of a grand portico of Corinthian columns, but also of use, becoming in turn the Royal Exchange, a public library (Stirling's Library) and then, in 1996, the Gallery of Modern Art. What had begun as a rich man's home, close enough to his place of business yet far enough west to put comfortable distance between him and the less salubrious environs of his workers, now stands, like so many of its contemporaries, firmly in the city centre.

George Square, the very hub of this city centre, is ringed with imposing façades, not least among them being that of the City Chambers, and dotted with statues of famous, as well as less

prominent, figures: Sir Walter Scott dominates the centre, looking down on Robert Burns, while Queen Victoria and her Prince Consort, Albert, sit on horseback at the far end, curiously enough with their backs to the City Chambers. But where is George in George Square? By 1781, when the square was being laid out, George III had been careless enough to lose the American Colonies, thus depriving Glasgow and the Tobacco Barons of a vital source of income and forfeiting his place of honour. Perhaps, however, there was at the time a certain poetic justice in retaining the name, since the square remained a hollow full of dirty water, on whose banks horses were slaughtered, until 1787, when building started on the fringes, continuing into the 1820s.

All around the square now lies the grid-pattern of the largely restored and refurbished New Town, or Merchant City, on which construction work began in the 1790s. The New Town was only briefly a residential quarter; when the fashionable merchants relocated their residences westwards, banks, markets and warehouses moved in. The city's financial heart also moved west in the mid

THE CITY CHAMBERS, George Square, opened in 1888 by Queen Victoria. The interior is resplendent with pillars and staircases in Carrara and Brescia marble and Scottish granite, mosaic floors and lavishly painted ceilings. The Chambers also contain a range of reception rooms, each panelled in a different wood, as well as a stunning Banqueting Hall.

*THE BOTANIC
GARDENS, since 1842
an oasis at the busy
junction of Great
Western Road, Queen
Margaret Drive and
Byres Road. In 1873, the
'Kibble Palace' glasshouse
was brought from
Coulport on the Clyde
Firth and re-assembled
here.*

nineteenth century, and the wholesale trades took over the area. It is still a layout unmatched anywhere in Britain, where each street, and each building in these streets, vies in architectural splendour with its neighbour.

The westward development started by Cunninghame and his contemporaries and taken up by their successors continued throughout the nineteenth century and into the early twentieth. From the city centre, along Great Western Road (which, from the Botanic Gardens, widens into a tree-lined boulevard in the grand manner) to Anniesland Cross is a long walk – and a rather noisy one in today's traffic conditions – but a rewarding one, presenting a vividly unfolding panorama of architectural styles in which the passage of the decades of the Victorian, Edwardian and subsequent eras is held in stone.

So indeed are many of Glasgow's notables themselves, back there on a hill, rising to 200 ft (61 m) on the opposite bank of the Molendinar Burn to the Cathedral. Owned since 1650 by the Merchants' House of Glasgow, the governing body of the Merchants'

Guild, this wooded hill, known as the Fir Park, was topped off in 1825 by a 70 ft (21 m) monument to John Knox (a nice irony, in view of the condign punishments the severe and stormy reformer had more than once called down on the then Rome-orientated congregation across the Burn). His image still looks down with clenched fist, but is now surrounded by what was Glasgow's first ecumenical burying-ground. A conscious imitation of the Père Lachaise cemetery in Paris, the Necropolis was opened in 1833 and contains a truly remarkable collection of ornate and opulent tombs and mausoleums, many of them blasted out of the rock. These last resting places of merchants, academics and other 'top people' of their times provide a reflection, in miniature, of the city's architectural wealth and diversity; clearly, their occupants enjoyed, in death, accommodation incomparably roomier and more luxurious than most of their fellow-citizens could have even dreamt of this side of the grave.

Any attempt to list the renowned architects involved in the construction of Glasgow and provide a detailed examination of their work would require a book in itself. Even in this exalted company,

WEST END comfort is reflected in the warmth of the red sandstone exterior of this typically stylish house in Dowanhill.

however, two names stand out: Charles Rennie Mackintosh and Alexander Thomson are notable not only on account of their superb works, but also because of the long neglect they endured in the city to which they contributed so much. There is perhaps something here of the typical Glasgow caution towards the local boy who makes good: the Glaswegian is fiercely proud of his city, but looks askance at anyone showing signs of getting above himself. Recent years have seen an upsurge in the appreciation of Mackintosh, but 'Greek' Thomson has still not been afforded the full respect which is his due. The refurbishing of his superb St Vincent Street Church and of Holmwood, a villa in Cathcart, under the umbrella of Glasgow 1999, City of Architecture and Design, may be first steps in this direction.

This pride is nothing new: even in the worst of times, it burned bright and hot. The city has always had to fight against its reputation (to which, it has to be said, it has also contributed). Many a foreign tourist guide-book has written Glasgow off as an 'ugly, dirty and violent industrial city best avoided'. It was once notorious for its fogs, some of them dense enough to stop even the usually reliable

CHARLES RENNIE MACKINTOSH
Two of Glasgow's finest examples of Mackintosh's individual style. The design for the Art Lover's House (above) won high praise in 1901, but the house was not built until the 1990s in Bella-houston Park. Glasgow School of Art (opposite), which opened in 1899, was designed when Mackintosh was only 28 and is considered his masterpiece.

ABOVE THE CITY looking east, a view impossible 50 years ago; industrial smog has given way to haze. The distinctive tower of the University is prominent (centre left).

STAINED GLASS in Hillhead.

trams, and its general blackness (for all that the name is reputed to derive from *gles chu*, 'the dear green place'; still, the city can boast over 70 parks), its poverty and its territorial gang warfare. And then, in 1990, Glasgow was the bearer of a proud new title, Cultural Capital of Europe, which turned into a year-long celebration, with thousands of events of all kinds, from internationally patronised concerts and exhibitions to street parties (Glaswegians never turn down any excuse for a good party!). It is no empty boast, no self-deluding loyalty when city authorities and ordinary citizens alike claim that Glasgow has always enjoyed a reputation as a City of Culture, an opinion also shared far beyond its boundaries.

Glasgow has long been in the forefront of culture, whether 'élite' or 'popular'. How else could Glaswegians not only survive in such a reputedly dark and depressing environment, but also earn a reputation for humour, hospitality and enjoyment of life? There has always been strong support for the two Glasgow-based orchestras, the Royal Scottish National and the BBC Scottish Symphony, and the regular visits by the Scottish

HILLHEAD DOORWAY, in the West End.

KELVINGROVE ART GALLERY AND MUSEUM

Chamber Orchestra to the City Halls and the Royal Concert Hall (opened in 1990), as well as the performances by Scottish Opera and Scottish Ballet in the Theatre Royal. Numerous amateur orchestras and choirs ensure that the interest in music is not merely passive, while the various annual festivals, such as the Jazz Festival and Celtic Connections among others, add their own flavours to the musical menu. The opening, in 1997, of the 3000-seat Clyde Auditorium (nicknamed 'the Armadillo' because of its distinctive shape) afforded a spectacular new venue for large-scale popular music events.

By far the liveliest sector of the cultural scene, however, formerly centred on the multiplicity of dance-halls and cinemas; in the years around the Second World War, Glasgow had 130 'picture houses', more per head than any other city outside the USA. Theatres flourished, mainly specialising in variety shows; the Glasgow Empire was renowned as either the making or the breaking of many an aspiring comedian, since the typically biting wit of the audience's heckling was often much funnier than the comic's material. Sadly, most of those palaces of popular entertainment have disappeared, fallen victim to the march of those twin tyrants, television and bingo – by no means an exclusively Glasgow phenomenon.

South of the Clyde, in Pollok Country Park, housed in its prize-winning building, stands a remarkable monument to one man's eclecticism, the Burrell Collection. Heir to an extensive merchant fleet, Sir William Burrell (1861-1958) was a self-trained art collector, and when he and his brother sold the business in 1916, he was able to devote his fortune to his collection, which he made over to the city of his birth in 1944.

THE BURRELL
A detail of this striking building in Pollok Country Park which houses Sir William Burrell's remarkable collection.

BRIDGES OVER THE RIVER CLYDE

THE GALLERY OF MODERN ART in Royal Exchange Square.

The Kelvingrove Art Gallery and Museum's collections (not only of paintings) enjoy an international reputation. It stands on the banks of the River Kelvin opposite the imposing University, which moved from the High Street in 1870 and now houses its own Hunterian Museum, a bequest of the celebrated anatomist, surgeon and obstetrician William Hunter (1718-1783). Across University Avenue, the Hunterian Art Gallery includes a reconstruction of the house in which Charles Rennie Mackintosh lived for nearly eight years. In addition to the numerous municipal establishments, many small private galleries also cater to the visual arts.

The city's own history is well documented in the People's Palace on Glasgow Green and in the Transport Museum across the road from the Kelvingrove Museum. What never ceases to amaze visitors, especially from abroad, is not only the range and quality of the exhibits themselves, but the large numbers of Glaswegians who regularly make an inspection of 'their' collections into a family outing.

And so, the picture of Glasgow, City of Culture, is almost complete. Almost, because to most Glaswegians, sport is an essential branch of culture. The clichéd view from outside sees Glasgow as

exclusively obsessed with football, and its populace neatly divided into two factions, swearing loyalty to the death (violent or otherwise) to either Celtic or Rangers. Like all clichés, this one falls well short of reality. There are in fact other groups, such as the neutrals who 'don't mind who beats Rangers or Celtic', those who have no interest in football whatsoever (they do exist!)... and that small band of stoics with an indomitable sense of black humour who support Partick Thistle. And then there are the followers of the many rugby clubs in the city or those who prefer to take their exercise on one of the 150 golf courses inside the city's boundaries or within 30 miles of its centre, some of which belong to private clubs, while others are open to the public.

City-dwellers with the urge to get out into the country are spoiled for choice and pampered by easy access. To the north and west, Loch Lomond, the Trossachs and the southernmost reaches of the Highlands lie within an hour's travel, as do the Firth of Clyde and the Ayrshire Coast to the south-west. In the days before anyone had so much as thought of package holidays or charter flights to the

THE PEOPLE'S PALACE, on Glasgow Green, houses a colourful social history of the city and its people. A favourite venue for a family day out.

THE FORMER TEMPLETON CARPET FACTORY, *Glasgow Green.*
The extravagant Venetian style earned it the nickname of the Doge's Palace.

It takes all sorts: hoarding on a building-site in Glassford Street.

Costa Brava, when the estuary was criss-crossed by the steamers of rival companies racing each other to pick up the passengers waiting on the next pier, this was the unchallenged holiday paradise for most Glaswegians. And for the majority of those taking part in the exodus down the river, or 'Doon the Watter', on the Friday in mid July that opened the general trades holiday fortnight of 'Glasgow Fair', there was only one way to go – by steamer. Changed days now: the Firth is as quiet as the upper reaches of the river, where over eighty different shipyards have long since fallen silent. With the construction of a number of marinas along the coast, the river and its estuary have become the playground of yachtsmen.

Glasgow has never been short of watering-holes, but whereas the pub was once an exclusively male domain, dark and cheerless, where respectable womenfolk would never have dreamt of setting foot in any case, most city-centre establishments now welcome all and also serve very acceptable bar meals. The elegant tea rooms which Charles Rennie Mackintosh designed for the celebrated Miss Cranston have long gone (only the Willow Tea Room in Sauchiehall Street remains, while a reproduction of the Buchanan Street one now stands next door to the original site), but modern successors can be found in

THE WILLOW TEA ROOM in Sauchiehall Street. The sole survivor of Charles Rennie Mackintosh's interiors for Miss Kate Cranston's popular chain of such establishments across the city centre.

PEACOCK DECORATION crowning the façade of Princes Square.

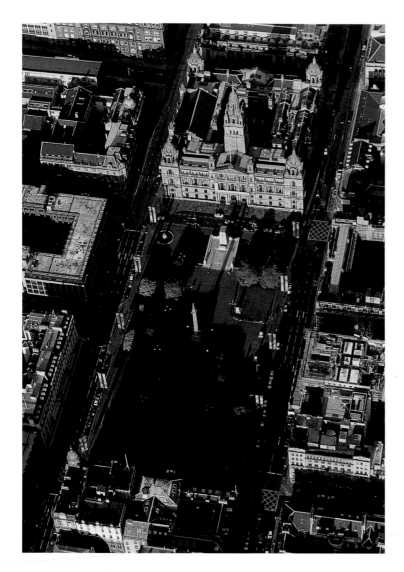

*GEORGE SQUARE &
THE CITY CHAMBERS
FROM THE AIR*

such oases as Princes Square and the Italian Centre in Ingram Street.

There is also a wide variety of restaurants on offer, specialising in Indian, Chinese, Italian, French and many other styles of cuisine, as well as traditional Scottish dishes.

For many, a natural concomitant of sightseeing is shopping, and here the all-weather shopper is well catered for, with three main malls within easy reach of each other: the St Enoch Centre at the foot of Buchanan Street, Princes Square a third of the way up and the new Buchanan Galleries at the top. While Glasgow's streets display the same national chain-store names as any other city, very often it is the architectural settings in which these familiar names are embedded that add a particular attraction.

Glasgow has come a long, and sometimes hazardous and bumpy way from St Mungo and his first church in that hamlet by the river to industrial metropolis, City of Culture in 1990 and City of Architecture and Design in 1999, but also from the bleakness of the dilapidated slums to the bright deter-mination of 'Glasgow's Miles Better', the city's slogan for the 1990s (miles better than it was, than its reputation and – than Edinburgh!). Glasgow has a vibrancy, as well as a nobility that has something monumental, but never bombastic, about it, and at the same time that 'lived-in' feel of a place that is first and foremost there for its inhabitants, whose character it reflects. If visitors come to see it, they are made thoroughly welcome, and the locals are unashamedly proud and delighted – and, of course, not in the least surprised – to hear them sing its praises. One of the most frequent comments heard, especially from foreign visitors, runs along the lines of: 'Well, I certainly didn't expect that!'

GLASGOW'S COAT OF ARMS, on a lamp-post at the People's Palace.
The tree, the fish, the bird and the bell all derive from the legend of St Mungo, also depicted here.

TENEMENTS, Dennistoun.

THE CITY CHAMBERS: the motto says it all.